Oxford Reading Tree
Dictionary

My name is

. . . .

OXFORD
UNIVERSITY PRESS

Great Clarendon Street, Oxford OX2 6DP

Oxford University Press is a department of the University of Oxford.
It furthers the University's objective of excellence in research,
scholarship,and education by publishing worldwide in

Oxford New York
Auckland Cape Town Dar es Salaam Hong Kong Karachi
Kuala Lumpur Madrid Melbourne Mexico City Nairobi
New Delhi Shanghai Taipei Toronto

With offices in
Argentina Austria Brazil Chile Czech Republic France Greece
Guatemala Hungary Italy Japan South Korea Poland Portugal
Singapore Switzerland Thailand Turkey Ukraine Vietnam

Oxford is a registered trade mark of Oxford University Press
in the UK and in certain other countries

Text copyright © Oxford University Press 2000
Illustrations copyright © Alex Brychta 2000
except p57 which is by Georgie Birkett
Roderick Hunt's and Alex Brychta's moral rights have been asserted

First published 2000/This edition 2008

This edition published exclusively for Scholastic Clubs and Fairs

British Library Cataloguing in Publication Data

Data available

ISBN 978-0-19-848788-3

10 9 8 7 6 5 4 3

Printed in Malaysia

Paper used in the production of this book is a natural,
recyclable product made from wood grown in sustainable
forests. The manufacturing process conforms to the
environmental regulations of the country of origin.

www.schooldictionaries.co.uk

TEACHERS
For inspirational support plus
free resources and eBooks
www.oxfordprimary.co.uk

PARENTS
Help your child's reading
with essential tips, phonics
support and free eBooks
www.oxfordowl.co.uk

Oxford Reading Tree
Dictionary

Illustrations by Alex Brychta

Main Consultant Roderick Hunt

Text compiled by Clare Kirtley

OXFORD

UNIVERSITY PRESS

For Dylan and Kelly *AB*
For Rosie *RH*
For Rose, Amy and Eleanor *CK*

Contents

Introduction

Oxford Reading Tree Dictionary uses the familiar characters and vocabulary from The Oxford Reading Tree Stages 1 to 5 to introduce children to the important features of a dictionary. It contains over 300 words, each word in the A to Z section being in alphabetical order with a simple definition and an interesting, colourful picture. There are also additional end sections with words that children will find particularly useful when writing, including all the key words from Stages 1 to 5. The words in the dictionary have been carefully chosen to support and develop children's reading, writing and speaking ability.

Here are the main features on the A to Z pages:

alphabet

capital letter

letter

symbol for verb

picture

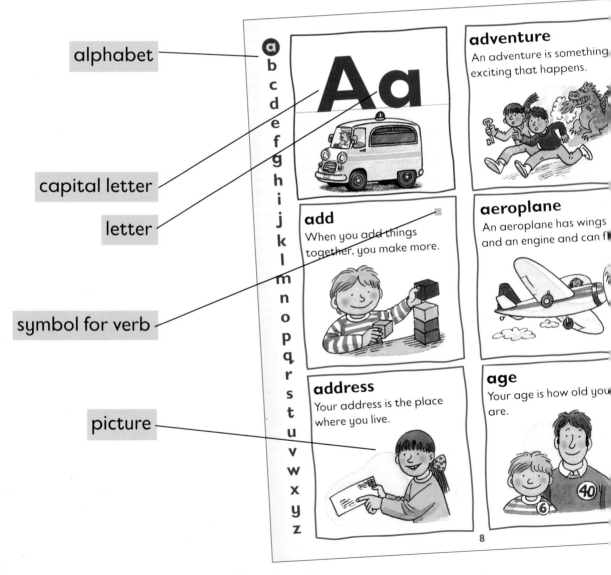

a b c d e f g h i j k l m n o p q r s t u v w x y z

Aa

adventure
An adventure is something exciting that happens.

add
When you add things together, you make more.

aeroplane
An aeroplane has wings and an engine and can f[...]

address
Your address is the place where you live.

age
Your age is how old you are.

8

6

Oxford Reading Tree Dictionary supports children's reading and understanding of The Oxford Reading Tree stories and helps children to acquire basic dictionary and reference skills in an enjoyable way. They can learn about the alphabet and alphabetical order, they can find out how to locate a word by using the initial letter, they can check their own spelling, and they can learn how to use simple definitions of words and so extend their vocabulary.

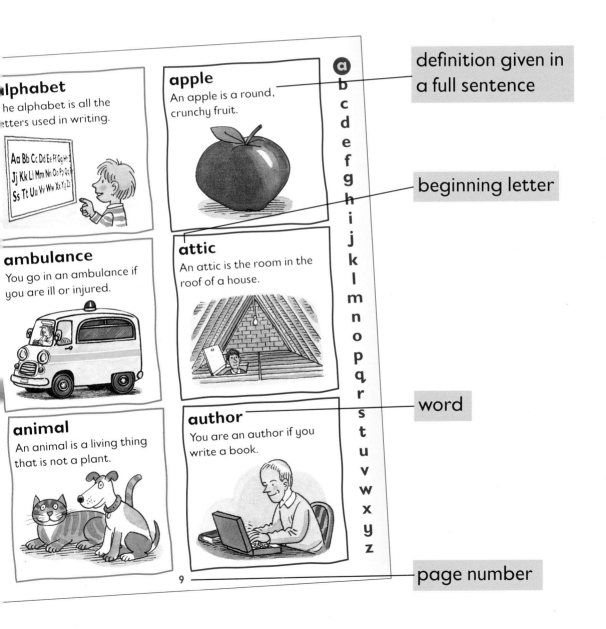

lphabet
he alphabet is all the
tters used in writing.

Aa Bb Cc Dd Ee Ff Gg Hh
Jj Kk Ll Mm Nn Oo Pp Qq
Ss Tt Uu Vv Ww Xx Yy Zz

apple
An apple is a round, crunchy fruit.

definition given in a full sentence

ambulance
You go in an ambulance if you are ill or injured.

attic
An attic is the room in the roof of a house.

beginning letter

animal
An animal is a living thing that is not a plant.

author
You are an author if you write a book.

word

a b c d e f g h i j k l m n o p q r s t u v w x y z

9

page number

a b c d e f g h i j k l m n o p q r s t u v w x y z

Aa

adventure

An adventure is something exciting that happens.

add

When you add things together, you make more.

aeroplane

An aeroplane has wings and an engine and can fly.

address

Your address is the place where you live.

age

Your age is how old you are.

alphabet

The alphabet is all the letters used in writing.

apple

An apple is a round, crunchy fruit.

ambulance

You go in an ambulance if you are ill or injured.

attic

An attic is the room in the roof of a house.

animal

An animal is a living thing that is not a plant.

author

You are an author if you write a book.

a b c d e f g h i j k l m n o p q r s t u v w x y z

Bb

balloon

A balloon is made from rubber. You blow it up.

baby

A baby is a very young child.

bark

A dog barks. It is a loud sound.

ball

A ball is round. You can play games with it.

bed

You sleep in a bed.

bedroom

A bedroom is a room you sleep in.

bird

A bird is an animal with wings, feathers and a beak.

bicycle

A bicycle has two wheels and you ride on it.

birthday

Your birthday is the day you were born.

big

An elephant is big to you.

boat

A boat floats on water.

book

A book has pages and a cover.

bridge

A bridge goes over a river, railway or road.

bounce

When you bounce a ball, it comes back up again.

bus

A bus takes people where they want to go.

box

A box holds things. It is often made from cardboard.

butterfly

A butterfly is an insect with four large wings.

Cc

castle

A castle is a large old building with thick walls.

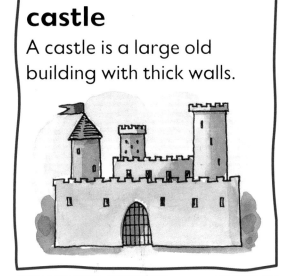

cake

A cake is a sweet food.

cat

A cat is a small furry animal.

car

A car has wheels and an engine.

chair

You sit on a chair.

climb

When you climb, you go up or down something.

computer

A computer stores information.

clown

A clown is someone who makes you laugh.

cook

You cook food by heating it.

coat

You wear a coat over your clothes when you go outside.

cross

If you are cross, you feel angry.

Dd

dog

A dog is an animal you can keep as a pet.

dance

When you dance, you move to music.

doll

A doll is a toy person.

day

You are awake during the day.

dolphin

A dolphin is an animal that lives in the sea.

a b c d e f g h i j k l m n o p q r s t u v w x y z

a b **c** d e f g h i j k l m n o p q r s t u v w x y z

door
You open a door to go into a room.

dream
When you dream, you see and hear things in your sleep.

dragon
A dragon is a fierce monster in stories.

drink
You can drink milk.

draw
You draw a picture with a pencil, pen or crayon.

drum
A drum makes a banging noise when you beat it.

Ee

egg

An egg has a thin hard shell.

ear

You use your ears to hear.

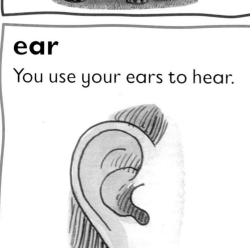

elephant

An elephant is a large animal with a trunk.

eat

You need to eat food to live.

eye

You use your eyes to see.

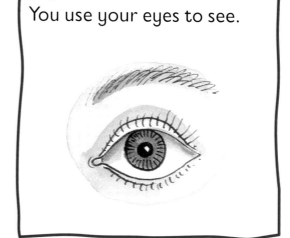

a b c d e f g h i j k l m n o p q r s t u v w x y z

a b c d e **f** g h i j k l m n o p q r s t u v w x y z

Ff

farm

A farm is where food is grown.

fair

You have fun at a fair.

feather

Birds have feathers instead of fur or hair.

fall

When you fall over, you hit the ground.

find

You need to look for something to find it.

fire

A fire is something burning. It is hot and bright.

flower

A flower is part of a plant.

fire engine

A fire engine is a lorry that is used to put out fires.

food

Food is what you eat to grow.

fish

A fish is an animal that lives under water.

frog

A frog is an animal with wet skin and webbed feet.

Gg

garden

You grow flowers and vegetables in a garden.

game

You play a game.

giant

If something is giant, it is very big.

garage

A car is kept in a garage.

giraffe

A giraffe is an animal with a long neck.

glasses

You wear glasses to help you see better.

goldfish

A goldfish is a small orange fish.

glow

When something glows, it gives off light and heat.

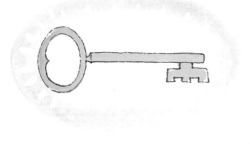

good

When you are good, people like you.

go-kart

A go-kart has four wheels and you ride on it.

guitar

A guitar is an instrument with strings.

a b c d e f **g** h i j k l m n o p q r s t u v w x y z

a b c d e f g **h** i j k l m n o p q r s t u v w x y z

Hh

happy

When you are happy, you feel good.

hair

Your hair grows on your head.

hat

You wear a hat on your head.

hand

Your hand has four fingers and a thumb.

head

Your eyes, ears and nose are on your head.

helicopter

A helicopter has blades that spin round on top.

hot

If something is hot, it can burn you.

holiday

A holiday is when you do not go to school or work.

house

You can live in a house.

hospital

You go to hospital if you are ill.

hungry

If you are hungry, you want to eat.

a b c d e f g **h** i j k l m n o p q r s t u v w x y z

Ii

idea

If you have an idea, you think of something.

ice

Freezing water turns to ice.

insect

An insect is a small animal with six legs.

ice cream

Ice cream is a very cold food that tastes like cream.

instrument

You use an instrument to make music.

Jj

journey
You travel from place to place on a journey.

jam
You make jam from fruit and sugar.

jug
You use a jug to pour a drink.

joke
A joke is a story that makes you laugh.

jump
When you jump, you go up into the air.

a b c d e f g h i **j** k l m n o p q r s t u v w x y z

Kk

king

Some countries are ruled by a king.

kettle

You use a kettle to boil water.

kitchen

You cook in a kitchen.

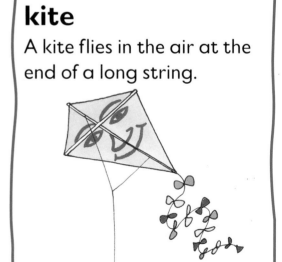

key

You use a key to unlock a door.

kite

A kite flies in the air at the end of a long string.

leaf

A leaf grows on a plant.

ladder

A ladder has rungs you can climb up and down.

letter

You write a letter to tell someone something.

Dear Wilf,

Please come to my party on Sunday.

Love,
Biff

laugh

You laugh when something is funny.

library

Books are kept in a library.

a b c d e f g h i j k **l** m n o p q r s t u v w x y z

a b c d e f g h i j k **l** m n o p q r s t u v w x y z

light

You need light to see. Light comes from a lamp.

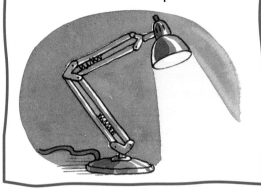

lock

A lock has a key to keep doors safely shut.

like

If you like someone, you think they are nice.

look

You use your eyes to look.

little

A mouse is little to you.

lose

If you lose something, you can not find it.

Mm

map

A map shows you how to get to places.

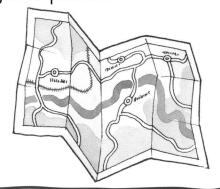

magic

Magic makes impossible things happen.

mend

You mend something which is broken.

make

You make something by putting things together.

milk

You can drink cow's milk.

a b c d e f g h i j k l m n o p q r s t u v w x y z

a b c d e f g h i j k l **m** n o p q r s t u v w x y z

mirror

You look at yourself in a mirror.

moon

You often see the moon in the sky at night.

money

You use money to buy things.

mountain

A mountain is a high hill.

monkey

A monkey is a furry animal that lives in trees.

mouse

A mouse is a small animal with a long tail.

Nn

new
Something is new when you first get it.

name
Your name is what people call you.

night
It is dark at night time.

nest
A bird lives in a nest.

nose
You use your nose to smell.

a b c d e f g h i j k l m **n** o p q r s t u v w x y z

Oo

open

You open a door.

octopus

An octopus is a sea creature with eight arms.

orange

An orange is a round fruit with thick peel.

old

You are old if you were born a long time ago.

owl

An owl is a bird which flies at night.

P p

pair

A pair is two things which go together.

page

A page is part of a book.

park

You can play in a park.

paint

You paint with a brush to colour a picture.

party

You have fun at a party with your friends.

a b c d e f g h i j k l m n o **p** q r s t u v w x y z

pencil
You use a pencil to write or draw.

pool
A pool has water in it.

photograph
You take a photograph with a camera.

pull
You can pull with your arms.

play
When you play, you have fun.

push
You push a wheelbarrow.

Qq

queue
You line up in a queue to wait for a bus.

queen
A queen is a woman who rules a country.

quick
You are quick when you move fast.

question
You ask a question to find out something.

quiet
You are quiet when you make very little noise.

Rr

rain

The rain is water falling from the sky.

rabbit

A rabbit is a small animal with long ears.

read

You read words written in books or on signs.

race

You run a race to find out who is the fastest.

recorder

A recorder is an instrument that you blow.

ride

You can ride a bicycle.

room

A room has walls and a door.

river

A river is a large stream of water.

rope

A rope is used to tie and pull things.

rocket

A rocket sends spacecraft into space.

run

When you run, you move your legs quickly.

a b c d e f g h i j k l m n o p q **r** s t u v w x y z

abcdefghijklmnopqr**s**tuvwxyz

Ss

sandwich

A sandwich is two slices of bread with food between them.

sad

You are sad when you feel unhappy.

school

You go to school to learn.

sand

Sand is very fine bits of rock. You find it by the sea.

shop

You buy things in a shop.

sleep

When you sleep, you close your eyes and rest.

story

A story is a made up adventure. You read stories in books.

snow

Snow is frozen rain that falls from the sky.

stream

A stream is a small river.

storm

A storm is a strong wind with rain or snow.

swing

A swing is a seat that moves backwards and forwards.

a b c d e f g h i j k l m n o p q r **s** t u v w x y z

a b c d e f g h i j k l m n o p q r s **t** u v w x y z

Tt

teddy

A teddy is a soft toy bear.

table

You sit at a table.

television

You watch and listen to things on television.

teacher

A teacher is a person who helps you to learn.

tent

You can sleep outside in a tent.

throw

You throw a ball through the air.

toy

You play with a toy.

toboggan

A toboggan slides along on snow.

tray

You carry things on a tray.

tooth

You use your teeth to bite and chew your food. A tooth can fall out.

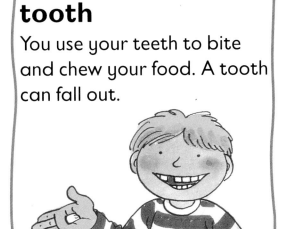

tree

A tree is a tall plant with leaves.

a b c d e f g h i j k l m n o p q r **s** **t** u v w x y z

41

Uu

uniform

The police and nurses wear a uniform.

ugly

If something is ugly, it is not nice to look at.

upset

When you are upset, you are not happy.

umbrella

An umbrella keeps you dry when it rains.

use

You use tools to make things.

Vv

vase
You put flowers in a vase.

van
A van can carry lots of things.

vegetable
A vegetable is a plant that you can eat.

vanish
If you vanish, you disappear.

video
A video records sound and pictures from the television.

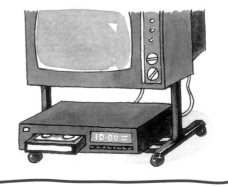

a b c d e f g h i j k l m n o p q r s t u v **w** x y z

Ww

water

Rivers and seas are made up of water.

wall

A wall is made of brick or stone.

weather

Snow, rain and sunshine are types of weather.

wash

You wash with soap and water to get clean.

wheel

A wheel turns round and round.

wind

The wind is air moving.

wood

A wood is where a group of trees grow.

window

A window is a space in a wall to let in light.

word

You use words when you speak or write.

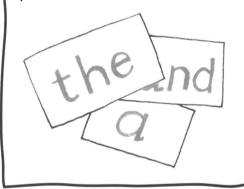

witch

A witch can do magic.

write

You write words for others to read.

a b c d e f g h i j k l m n o p q r s t u v **w** x y z

Xx

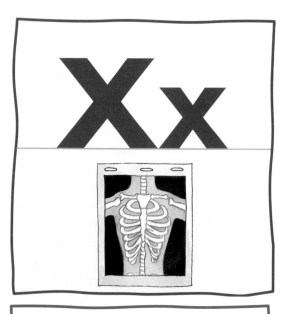

Yy

X-ray

An X-ray shows the inside of your body.

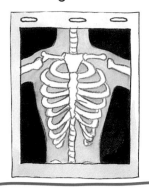

yawn

You yawn when you are tired.

xylophone

A xylophone is an instrument with wooden or metal bars.

year

There are twelve months in a year.

yell

When you yell, you shout loudly.

yogurt

You make yogurt from sour milk.

young

You are young if you were born a short time ago.

Zz

zebra

A zebra is an animal with black and white stripes.

zoo

You can see wild animals at a zoo.

Friends from The Oxford Reading Tree

Anneena

Chip

Floppy

Biff

Dad

Gran

Kipper

Mum

Wilf and Wilma

Mrs. May

Nadim

49

Some useful words for writing

a
about
adventure
after
again
all
am
an
and
another
are
as
at
away

back
ball
barked
be
because
bed
been
began
big
box
boy
brother
but
by

called
came
can
can't
cat
children
climbed
come
could
couldn't
cross

dad
day
did
dig
do
dog
don't
door
down

everyone

first
for
found
frightened
from

gave
get
girl
glowing
go
going
good
got

had
half
has
have
he
help
helped
her
here
him
his
home
house
how

I
if
in
inside
is
it
it's

jump
jumped
just

key

last
laugh
like
liked
little
lived
look
looked
love

made
magic
make
man
many
may
me
mended
more
much
mum
must
my

name
new
next
night
no
not
now

of
off
old
on
once
one
opened
or
our
out
outside
over

painted
people
picked
play
played
pull
pulled
push
pushed
put

ran
room

said
saw
school
see
seen
she
should
sister
so
some
storm

take
than
that
the
their
them
then
there
these
they
things
this
three
threw
time
to
told
too
took
tree
turned
two

up
us

very

wallpaper
want
wanted
was
water
way
we
went
were
what
when
where
who
will
with
would

yelled
yes
you
your

Verbs (These are doing words)

add

added

call

called

draw

drew

bark

barked

climb

climbed

dream

dreamed

bounce

bounced

cook

cooked

drink

drank

buy

bought

dance

danced

eat

ate

fall

fell

help

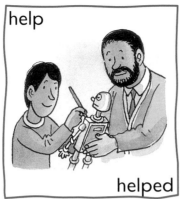

helped

look

looked

find

found

jump

jumped

lose

lost

give

gave

laugh

laughed

make

made

glow

glowed

like

liked

mend

mended

open

opened

pull

pulled

run

ran

paint

painted

push

pushed

say

said

pick

picked

read

read

see

saw

play

played

ride

rode

sleep

slept

take
took

use
used

wash
washed

tell
told

vanish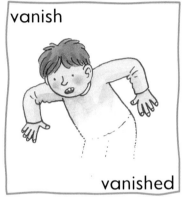
vanished

write
wrote

throw
threw

walk
walked

yawn
yawned

turn
turned

want
wanted

yell
yelled

Days of the week

Sunday

Monday

Tuesday

Wednesday

Thursday

Friday

Saturday

Months of the year

January

July

February

August

March

September

April

October

May

November

June

December

Numbers

0

zero

1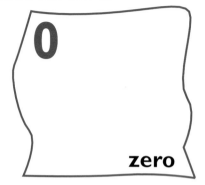

one

2

two

3

three

4

four

5

five

6

six

7  seven

8  eight

9  nine

10  ten

11  eleven

12  twelve

13  thirteen

14
fourteen

15
fifteen

16
sixteen

17
seventeen

18
eighteen

19
nineteen

20
twenty

Colours

black

blue

brown

green

grey

orange

pink

purple

red

white

yellow

61

The alphabet

Aa

Ee

Bb

Ff

Cc

Gg

Dd

Hh

Ii

Jj

Kk

Ll

Mm

Nn

Oo

Pp

Qq

Rr

Ss

Tt

Uu

Vv

Ww

Xx

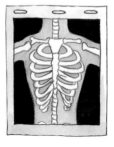

Yy

Zz